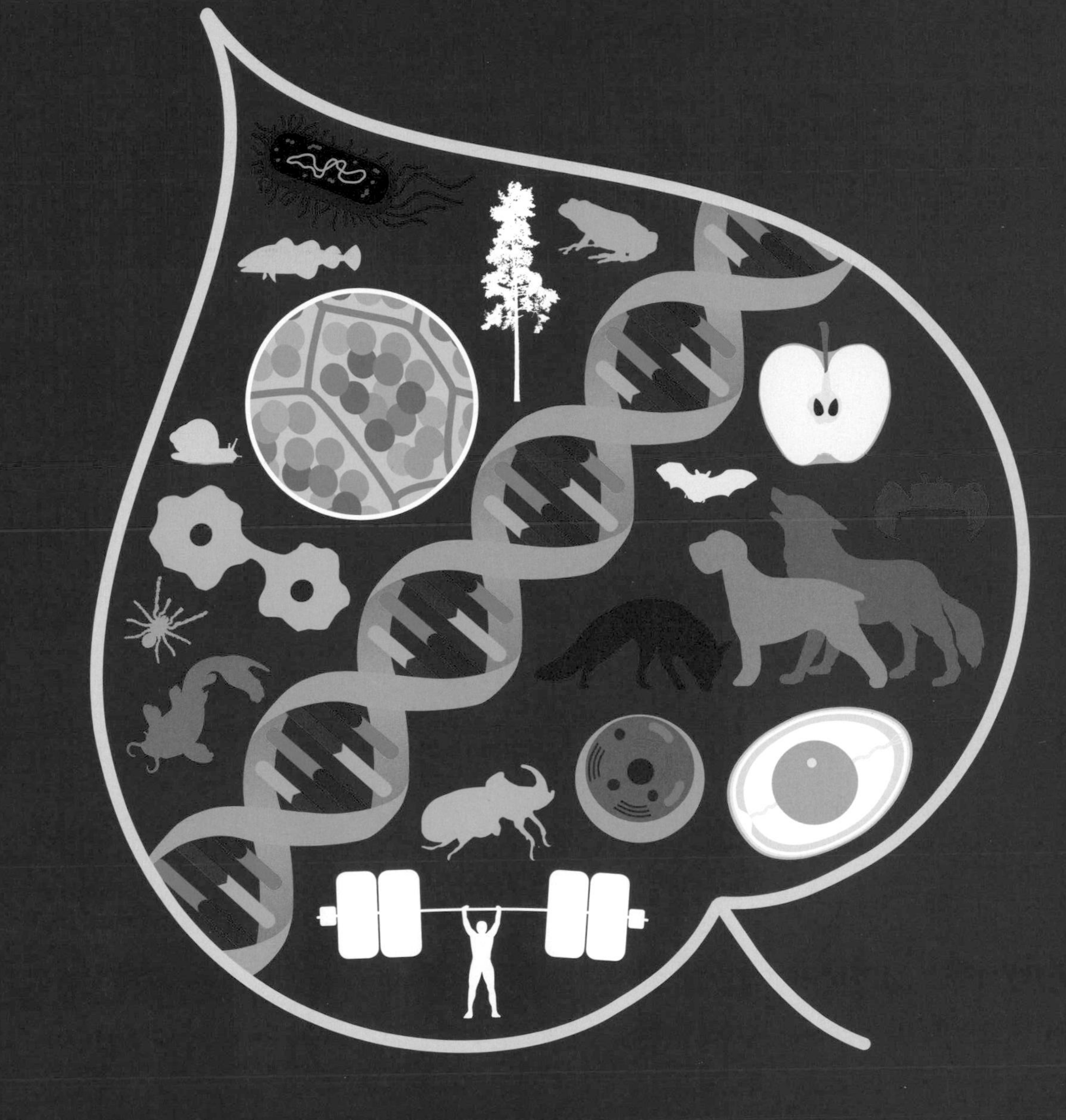

CONTENTS

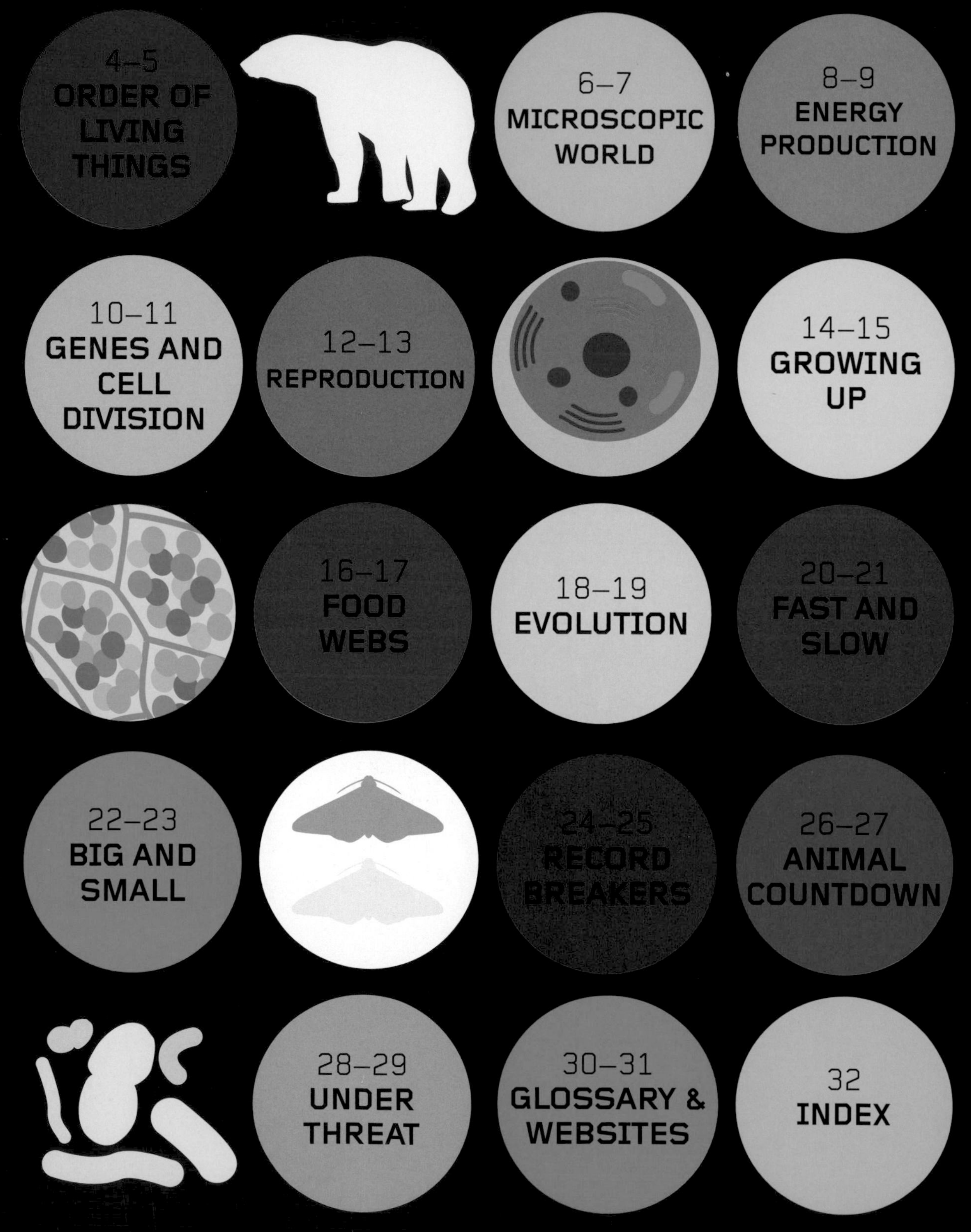

WELCOME TO THE WORLD OF INFOGRAPHICS

Using icons, graphics and pictograms, infographics visualise data and information in a whole new way!

BE AMAZED BY THE REAL-LIFE SIZE OF THE WORLD'S LARGEST SPIDER

DISCOVER WHICH ANIMAL CAN JUMP THE EQUIVALENT OF A HUMAN LEAPING OVER A SKYSCRAPER!

FIND OUT WHICH ANIMAL WOULD WIN THE GOLD MEDAL IN A SPRINT RACE

MEASURE THE LENGTH OF A BLUE WHALE IN BUSES, PEOPLE AND BASKETBALL COURTS

ORDER OF LIVING THINGS

Our planet is teeming with billions of organisms, from microscopic algae to gigantic whales. In order to identify each living thing, scientists use a classification system.

KINGDOMS

ANIMALS

PLANTS

FUNGI

PROTISTS
(MICRO-ORGANISMS)

EUBACTERIA
(MICRO-ORGANISMS)

ARCHEOBACTERIA
(MICRO-ORGANISMS)

CLASSIFICATION

All living things belong to one of six kingdoms. Each kingdom is divided into groups, from phylum down to species. The graphic shows how a species, in this case the wolf, is identified using this classification system.

INSECTS OUTNUMBER HUMANS BY

200,000,000 TO 1

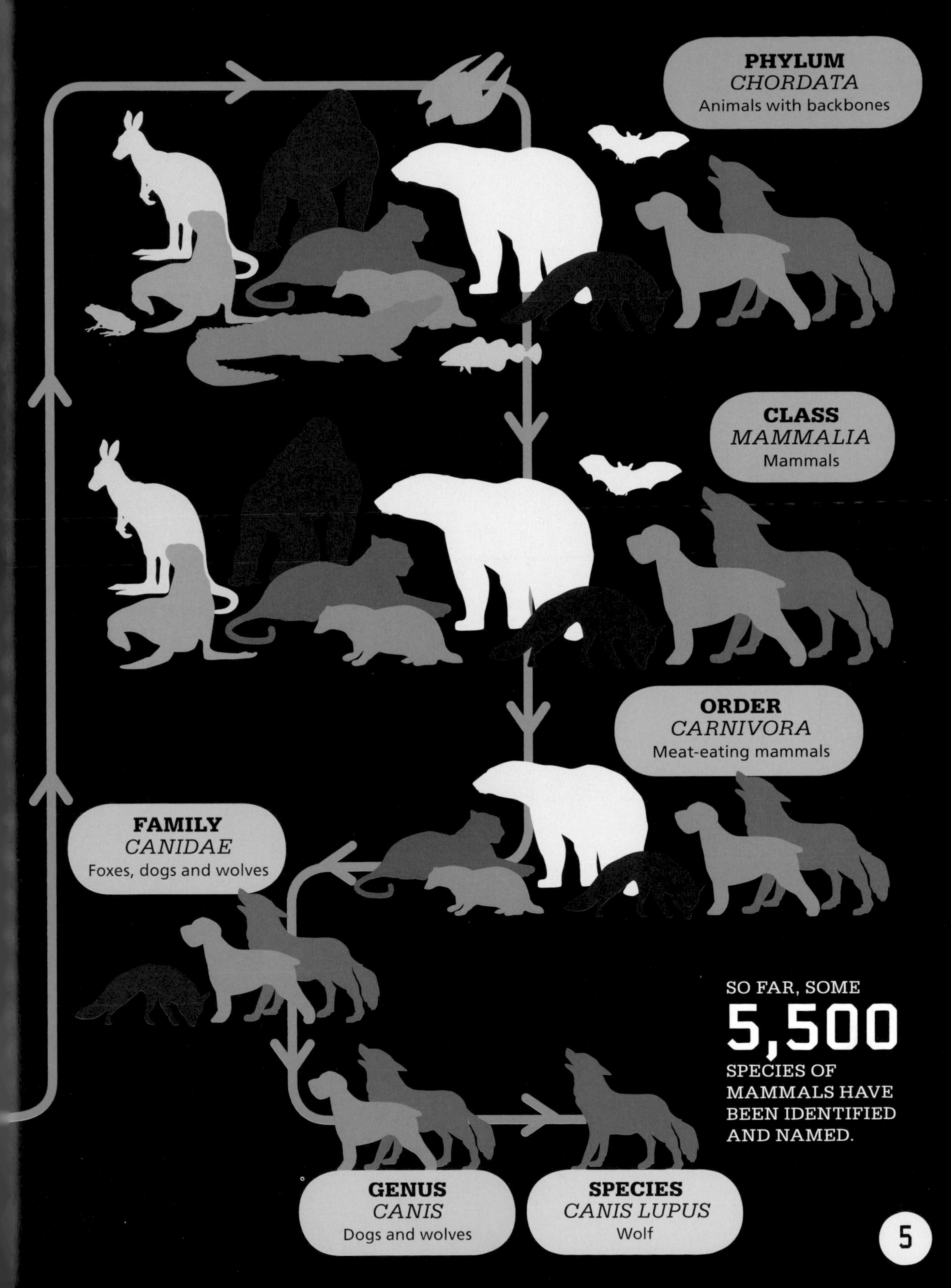

SO FAR, SOME **5,500** SPECIES OF MAMMALS HAVE BEEN IDENTIFIED AND NAMED.

MICROSCOPIC WORLD

There are entire kingdoms of micro-organisms that are too small to see with the naked eye. For example, a single gram of soil can contain 40 million bacteria alone!

BIGGEST KILLERS

The number of people killed each year by various diseases caused by micro-organisms.

3.9 MILLION
LOWER RESPIRATORY INFECTIONS (SUCH AS PNEUMONIA)

2.8 MILLION
HIV/AIDS

1.8 MILLION
DIARRHEAL DISEASES

1.6 MILLION
TB

1.3 MILLION
MALARIA

0.6 MILLION
MEASLES

400 NANOMETRES

The size of the largest viruses – about 1/250th the width of a human hair.

BREAD

Not all micro-organisms are harmful. Humans use some in food and drink and to treat waste. For example, yeast is used in bread-making to turn the sugars in bread dough into tiny bubbles of carbon dioxide, making the bread 'rise'.

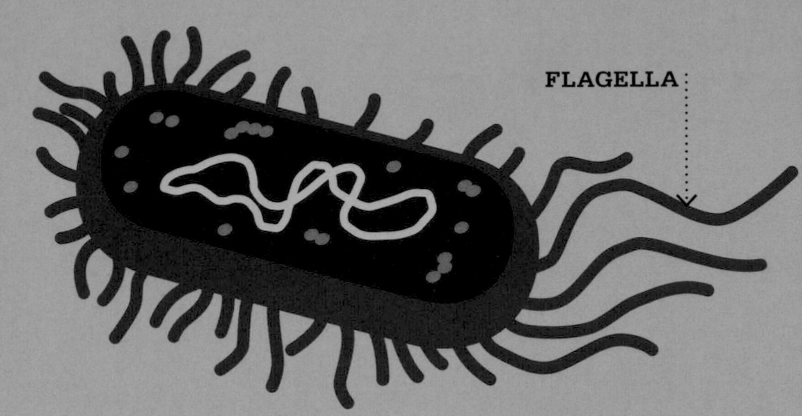

CELLS

All organisms are made up of cells. Micro-organisms often consist of one cell, while plants and animals are made up of billions. Prokaryotic cells are those that do not contain a cell nucleus. They include bacteria, some of which have flagella, which they wiggle to move about.

NUCLEUS

NUCLEUS

PLANT CELL

EUKARYOTIC

Eukaryotic cells contain a cell nucleus, inside which is the genetic information for the cell. Plants and animals are formed from two different types of eukaryotic cells.

ANIMAL CELL

About 10,000 human cells could fit onto the head of a pin

10,000

THE LARGEST KNOWN CELLS ARE UNFERTILISED OSTRICH EGGS.

They weigh about 1.6 kg – nearly two bags of sugar.

CHICKEN EGG

ALLIGATOR EGG

TURTLE EGG

HUMMINGBIRD EGG

ENERGY PRODUCTION

The Sun is the source of most of the energy used on our planet. Plants convert this energy into substances that all living things can then use to produce energy to survive and grow.

LIGHT ENERGY FROM THE SUN

CHLOROPHYLL

WATER

CARBON DIOXIDE

PHOTOSYNTHESIS

Chlorophyll is found inside many plant cells. It plays an important part in harnessing sunlight during a process called photosynthesis. This process converts water and the gas carbon dioxide into sugars and oxygen.

WITH OR WITHOUT

Respiration that uses oxygen is called aerobic, while respiration that does not use oxygen is called anaerobic.

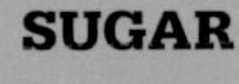

EACH YEAR, ONE HECTARE OF TREES CONSUMES THE SAME AMOUNT OF CARBON DIOXIDE PRODUCED BY AN AVERAGE CAR THAT HAS BEEN DRIVEN FOR

100,000 KM

That same hectare of trees also produces enough oxygen for

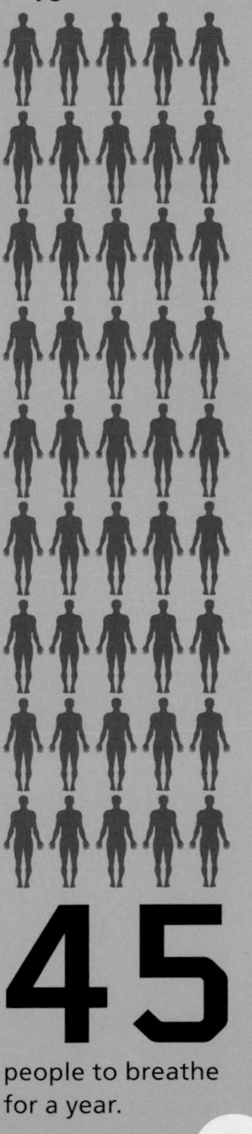

45

people to breathe for a year.

RESPIRATION

During respiration, sugars are used to produce energy. Tiny structures called mitochondria found in cells are the main sites for this energy production. As well as producing energy, this process also creates the gas carbon dioxide and water.

GENES AND CELL DIVISION

Every organism contains instructions that determine how it looks and behaves. These instructions are stored on a long, twisted molecule called DNA.

BASE PAIR

GUANINE

ADENINE

THYMINE

PHOSPHATE
BACKBONE

DNA MOLECULE

A DNA molecule consists of two twisting backbones, which are joined together by chemicals that are linked in pairs, called base pairs. These pairs are organised into certain sequences, called genes, and these determine how an organism acts.

There are an estimated 3 billion DNA bases in the human genome.

3,000,000,000

CHROMOSOMES

Chromosomes are structures found inside cells. They are made up of long strands of DNA that are twisted and coiled together tightly.

If it was unravelled, the **DNA** from a single **cell** in a **human body** would be approximately **2 metres** long – that's taller than most humans!

HUMANS AND CHIMPS SHARE UP TO

95%

OF THEIR DNA

CELL DIVISION

Cells divide in order to multiply. To do this, they need to duplicate their genetic information before splitting apart.

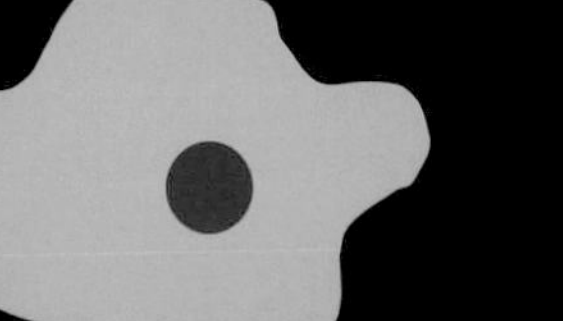

1. PARENT CELL

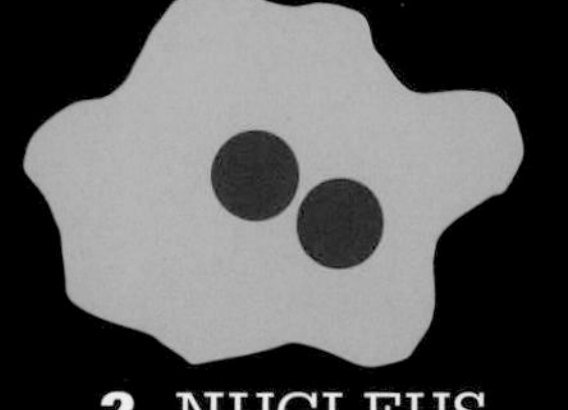

2. NUCLEUS DIVIDES

3. CELL SPLITS

4. TWO DAUGHTER CELLS

REPRODUCTION

All living things reproduce, so that their species can survive. Reproduction can be asexual, whereby one organism duplicates itself, or sexual, whereby cells from two organisms join together to produce young.

ASEXUAL REPRODUCTION

Some simple organisms, such as amoeba, will simply divide in two. Others, such as this hydra, reproduce by budding, creating an identical, but smaller, version of themselves.

BUD

FLOWERS AND SEEDS

Plants contain male cells, called pollen, stored in anthers, and female cells inside an ovary. The two cells join together to form seeds. Some seeds, such as the pips in an apple, are surrounded by fruit. Animals eat the fruit and the seeds are spread in the animals' dung. Sycamore seeds have a special wing shape, which allows them to spin away from the parent plant and spread.

PETAL
STIGMA
ANTHER
STYLE
FILAMENT
OVARY
SEED WINGS
SYCAMORE SEEDS

APPLE SEEDS

FRUIT

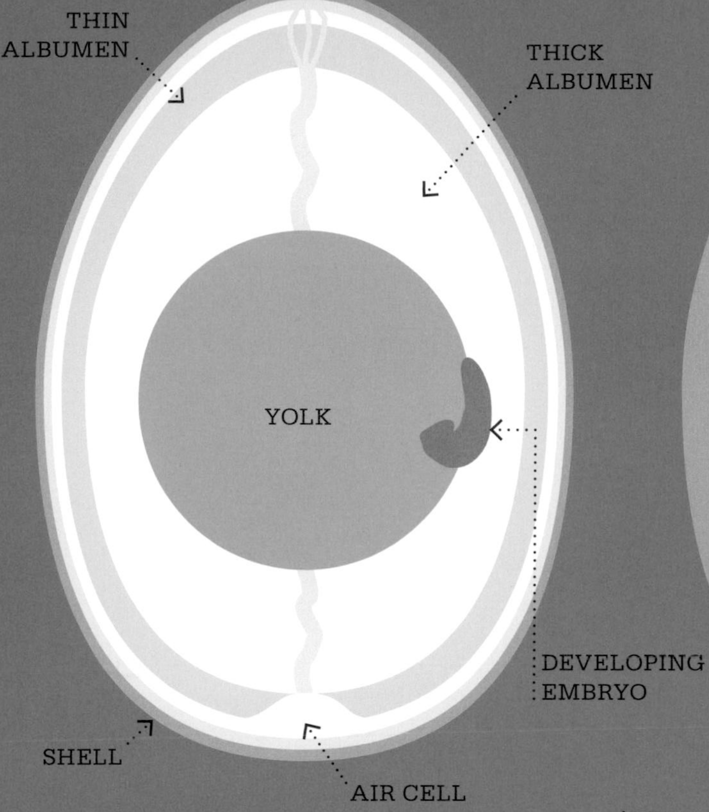

LAYING EGGS

Many animals lay eggs which contain the developing young. Inside a chicken's egg, the developing young, or embryo, is fed by nutrients in the yolk, while being supported and protected by the albumen.

FEMALE ELEPHANT **3,000 KG**

LIVE BIRTH

The young of mammals develop inside the mother's uterus. This development period is called the gestation. Over time, the young will develop and grow until they are old enough to be born.

22 MONTHS

GESTATION PERIOD FOR AN ELEPHANT – THE LONGEST OF ANY LAND ANIMAL.

CALF
105 KG

RABBITS HAVE A FAST BREEDING RATE. IN A SINGLE BREEDING SEASON, A PAIR CAN MULTIPLY TO AS MANY AS **800** RABBITS OVER THREE OR FOUR GENERATIONS.

GROWING UP

As a plant or animal gets older, it grows and matures before it finally dies. During its life span, it may go through many stages, including a complete change in body shape and form.

HOW LONG CAN ANIMALS LIVE?

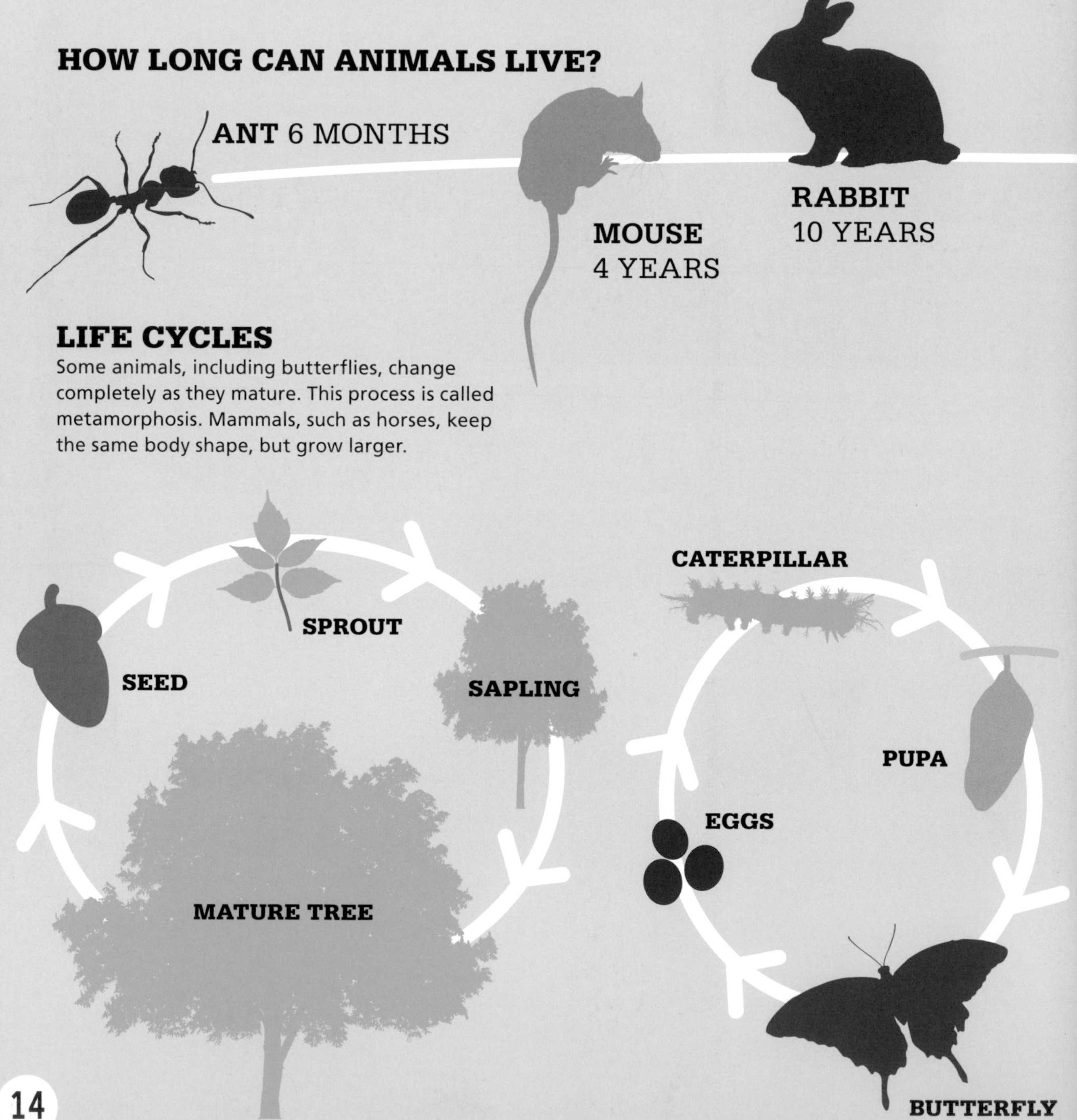

LIFE CYCLES

Some animals, including butterflies, change completely as they mature. This process is called metamorphosis. Mammals, such as horses, keep the same body shape, but grow larger.

A **Great Basin Bristlecone pine** in North America is the **oldest** known living individual tree. Samples from its core and rings show that it is more than **4,800 years old.**

BOTTLENOSE DOLPHIN
45 YEARS

HORSE
30 YEARS

KOI CARP
70 YEARS

ASIAN ELEPHANT
60 YEARS

HUMAN
70–80 YEARS

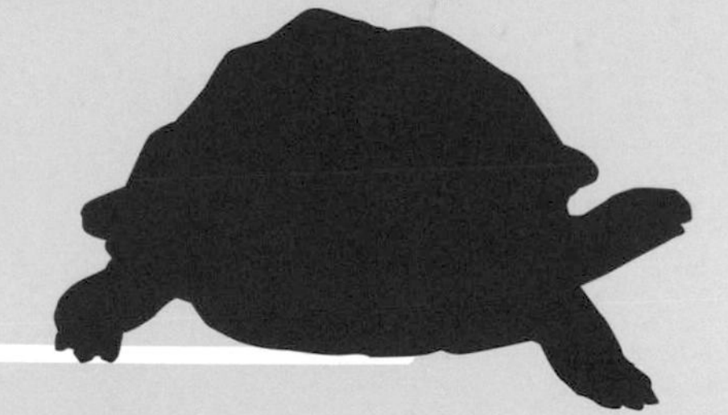

GALAPAGOS TORTOISE
190 YEARS

4,265

A type of black coral called Leiopathes is one of the oldest continuously living organisms. Some specimens of the coral are around 4,265 years old.

FOOD WEBS

Most energy comes from the Sun. This energy is harnessed by plants and passed on when they are eaten by animals, who are, in turn, eaten by their predators. This relationship is called a food chain.

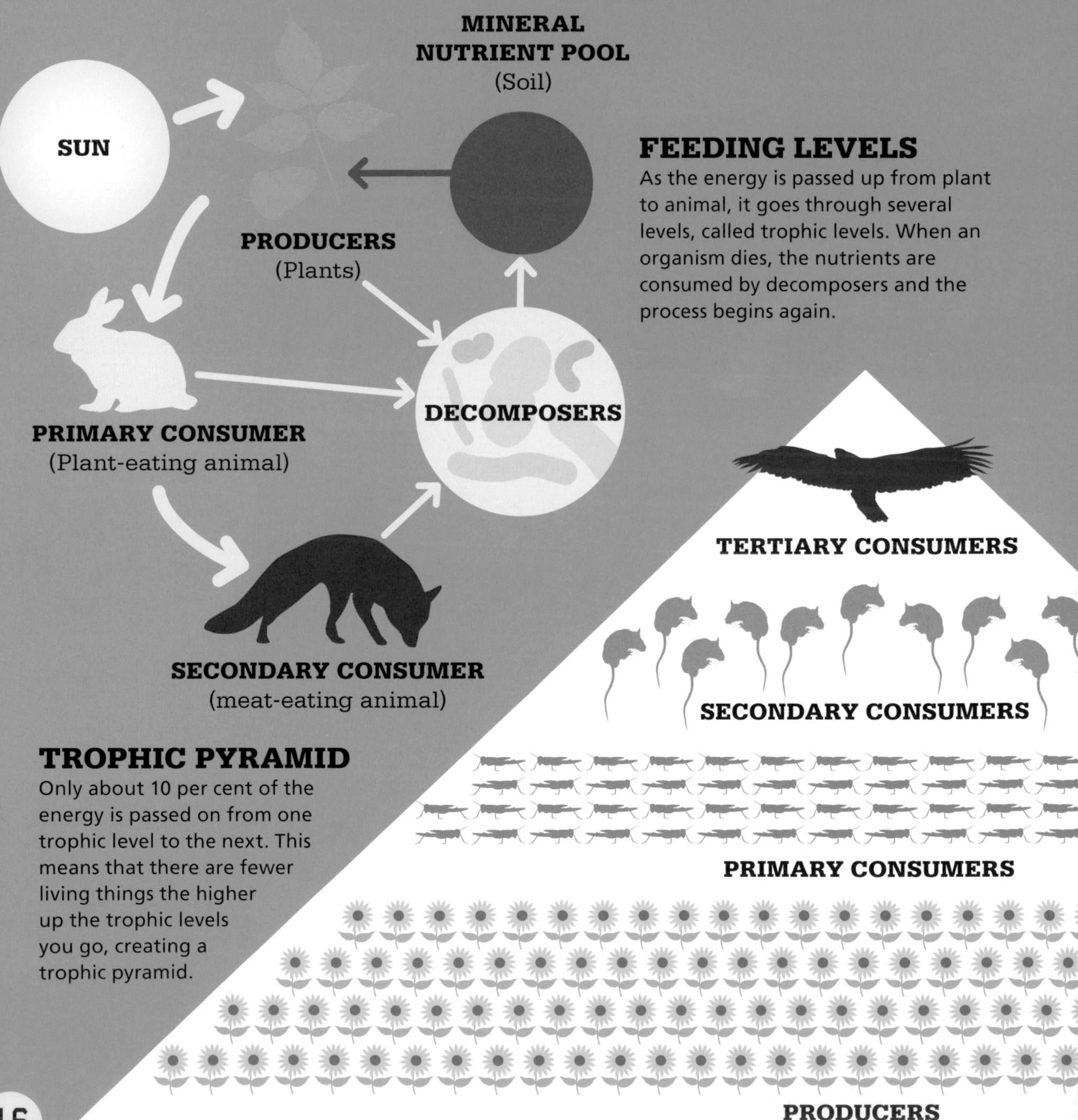

FEEDING LEVELS

As the energy is passed up from plant to animal, it goes through several levels, called trophic levels. When an organism dies, the nutrients are consumed by decomposers and the process begins again.

TROPHIC PYRAMID

Only about 10 per cent of the energy is passed on from one trophic level to the next. This means that there are fewer living things the higher up the trophic levels you go, creating a trophic pyramid.

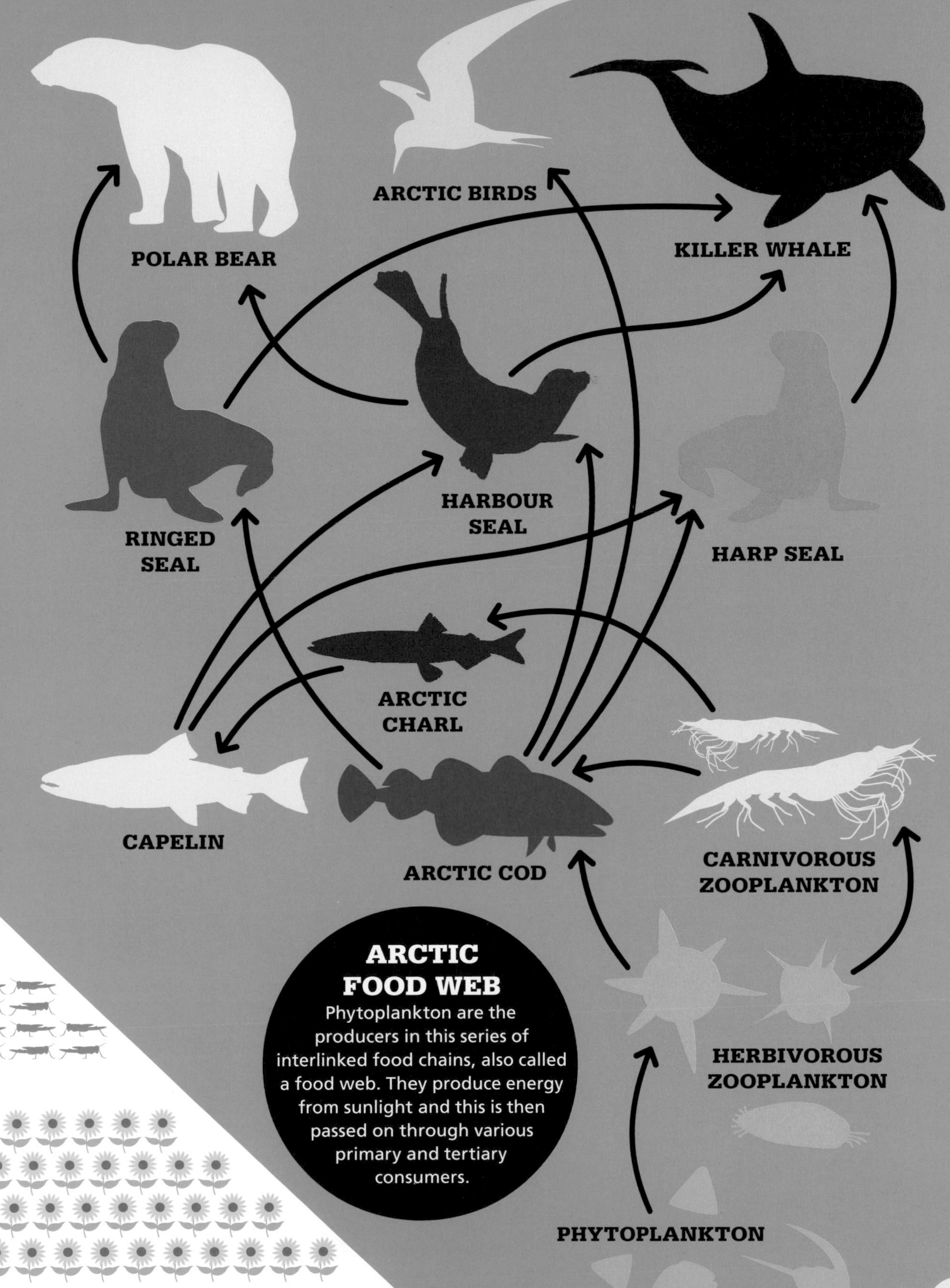

ARCTIC FOOD WEB

Phytoplankton are the producers in this series of interlinked food chains, also called a food web. They produce energy from sunlight and this is then passed on through various primary and tertiary consumers.

EVOLUTION

Throughout the history of the Earth, new species have appeared while others have died out or changed. This process is called evolution and it occurs in response to changing conditions on our planet.

MOTH

The peppered moth has changed as its habitat has altered. During the 19th century, pollution from factories darkened tree barks. This meant that light versions of the moth were easy to spot by predators. Dark varieties made up a tiny amount of peppered moths at the start of the 19th century. By 1900, they made up more than 95 per cent.

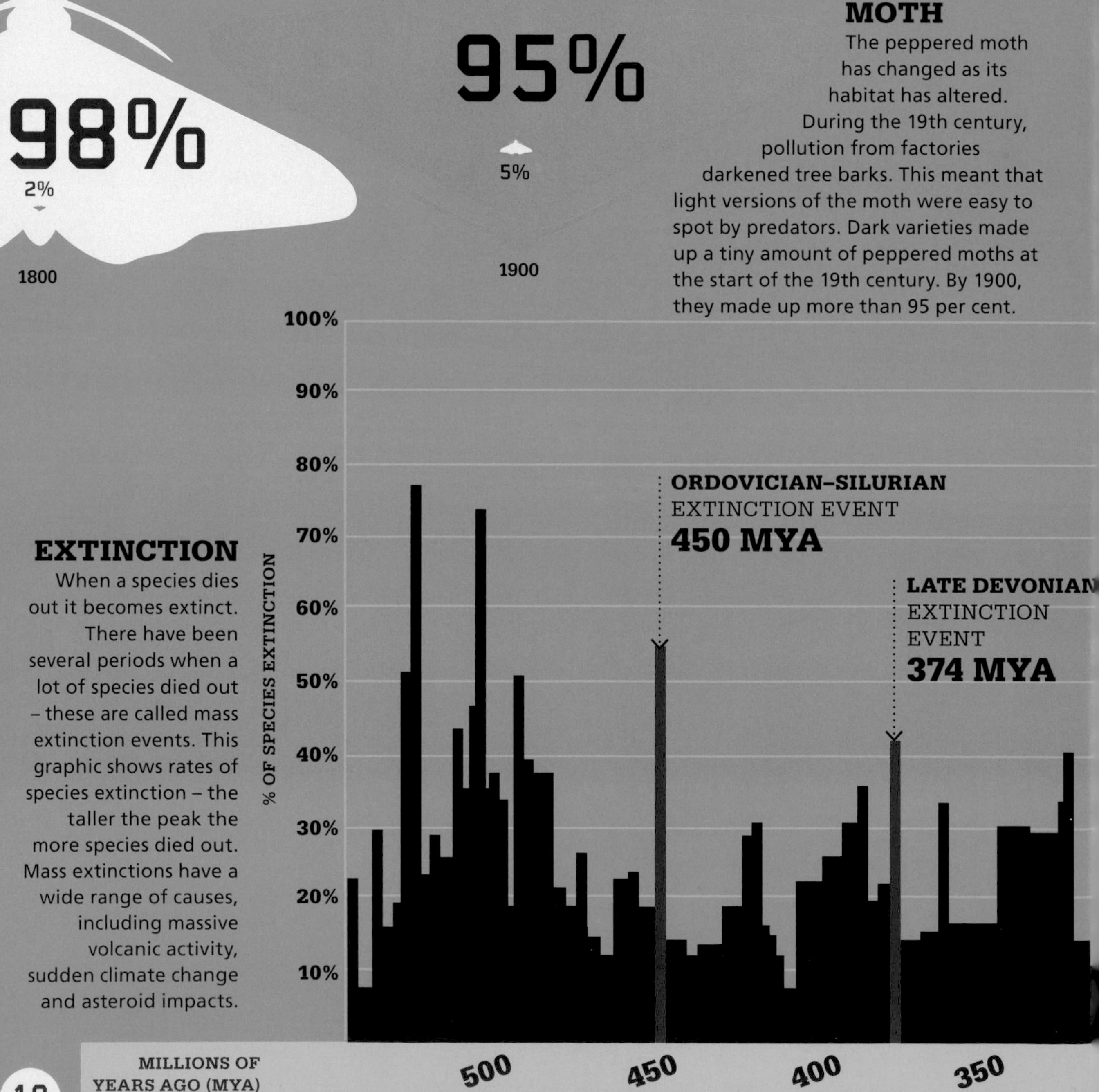

EXTINCTION

When a species dies out it becomes extinct. There have been several periods when a lot of species died out – these are called mass extinction events. This graphic shows rates of species extinction – the taller the peak the more species died out. Mass extinctions have a wide range of causes, including massive volcanic activity, sudden climate change and asteroid impacts.

FINCHES

British scientist Charles Darwin developed the theory of evolution by studying animal life on the Galapagos Islands in the Pacific. Here, he noticed that various species of finches had differently shaped beaks to suit the types of food they ate.

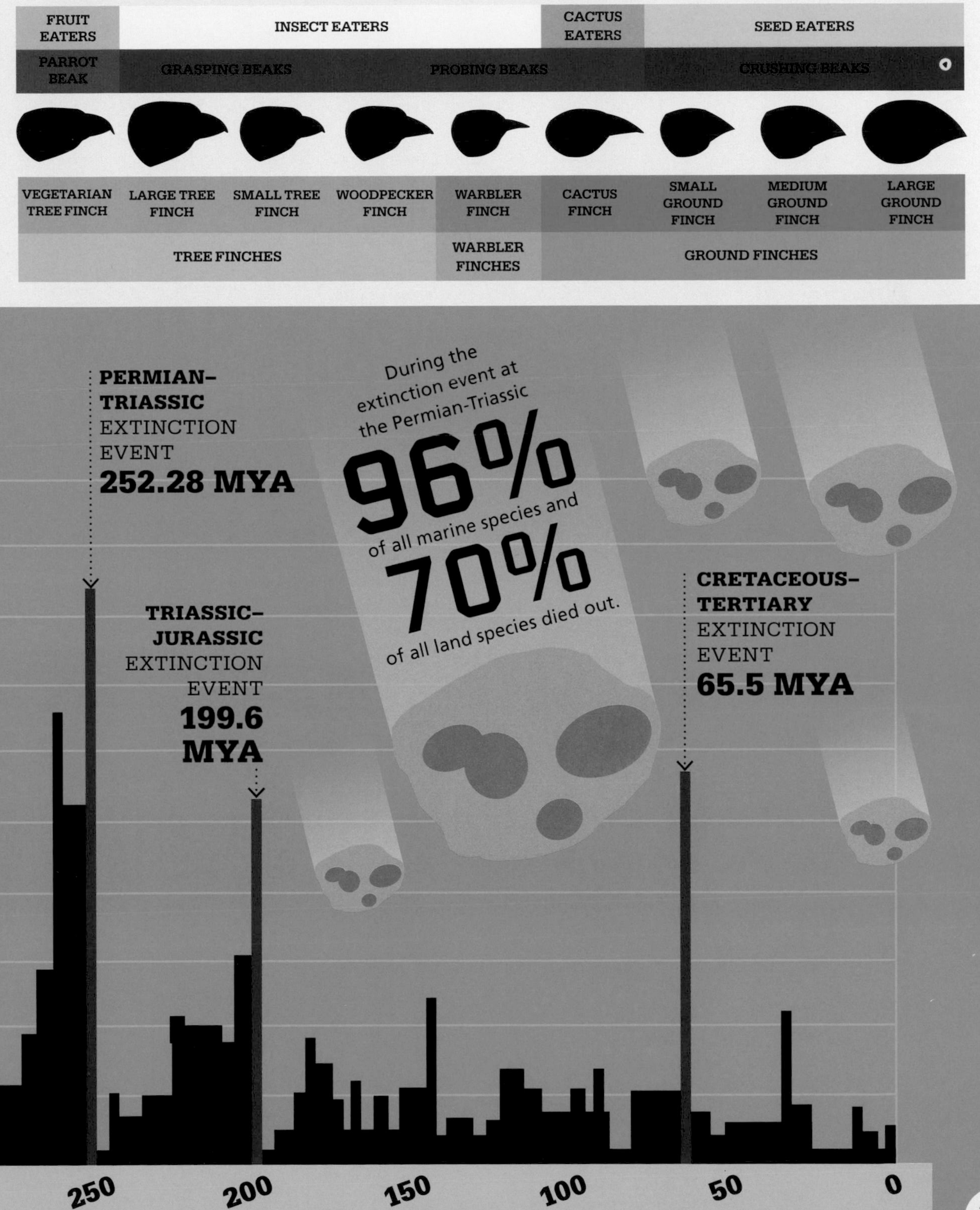

FAST AND SLOW

Living beings often use speed for survival, for example to outrun a predator. Other organisms live at a slower pace in order to save energy.

The fastest accelerating living thing on the planet is the hat thrower fungus. The spores are released on a jet of liquid with an acceleration of

0–32 KM/H IN JUST 2 MILLIONTHS OF A SECOND

experiencing forces of 20,000G – astronauts blasting into space only experience 4G.

FASTEST ANIMALS

PEREGRINE FALCON
320 KM/H

SPEED

AUSTRALIAN TIGER BEETLES
CAN REACH SPEEDS OF 6.7 KM/H WHEN ESCAPING PREDATORS. BUT THEY ARE ONLY 1 CM LONG, SO THEY TRAVEL AT ABOUT

170 BODY LENGTHS PER SECOND.

IF AN OLYMPIC SPRINTER COULD MATCH THAT RATE OF BODY LENGTHS PER SECOND, THEY WOULD BE RUNNING AT NEARLY

1,200 KM/H – THAT'S FASTER THAN THE SPEED OF SOUND AT SEA LEVEL!

SLOWEST ANIMALS
GARDEN SNAIL
0.03 KM/H
GIANT TORTOISE
0.3 KM/H
IN ONE MINUTE A GARDEN SNAIL CAN TRAVEL
5 CM
SEAHORSE
0.02 KM/H
IN ONE HOUR THEY CAN GROW
4 CM
Some species of bamboo are the fastest growing plants in the world, capable of growing 1 metre in a single day
SWORDFISH AND MARLIN
100 KM/H
FASTEST FISH
HORSE
70 KM/H
HUMAN SPRINTER
37.5 KM/H
CHEETAH 120 KM/H
FASTEST LAND ANIMAL
WOLF 65 KM/H
AT THIS SPEED, THE AUSTRALIAN TIGER BEETLE WOULD COMPLETE 100 METRES IN JUST
0.3 SECONDS.
AN OLYMPIC SPRINTER TAKES 10 SECONDS TO RUN 100 METRES.

BIG AND SMALL

Whether they reach super-size proportions or can pass through the eye of a needle, these record-breaking organisms have found their own way of surviving in the world.

A **giant fungus** of the honey mushroom species covers **8.9 sq km** of land in Oregon, USA, making it the **largest** ever known organism by area.

GIRAFFE
6 M

Standing next to some of the tallest animals in the world, the average human is a little short. Top of the tree are giraffes, which can reach more than three times an average person's height.

ELEPHANT **4 M**

OSTRICH **2.75 M**

MAN
1.8 M

HORSE
2.2 M

THE BLUE WHALE IS THE LARGEST ANIMAL EVER

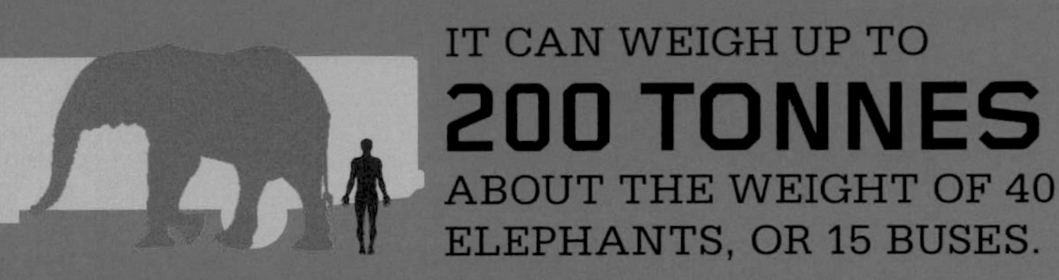

IT CAN WEIGH UP TO

200 TONNES

ABOUT THE WEIGHT OF 40 ELEPHANTS, OR 15 BUSES.

30 M LONG Which is about the same length as 17 people, 3 school buses or a basketball court.

It can eat up to four tonnes of krill in a day.

ITS TONGUE CAN WEIGH AS MUCH AS AN ELEPHANT.

A newborn blue whale puts on about 90 kg of weight every single day during its first year.

SMALLEST FLOWERING PLANT

GENUS WOLFIA

An individual plant is just 0.6 mm long and 0.3 mm wide.

ACTUAL SIZE

BIGGEST FLOWER

RAFFLESIA ARNOLDII

It measures up to 1 metre across and gives off an odour of decaying flesh.

CAMEL **2.15 M**

TALLEST TREE

ACTUAL SIZE

GREATEST JUMPER

The froghopper is the world's greatest jumper. It can leap 70 cm into the air, but it's only 0.6 cm long.

THAT IS THE SAME AS A PERSON LEAPING OVER A 210-METRE HIGH SKYSCRAPER!

RECORD BREAKERS

The creatures on these pages have developed some amazing ways of surviving, whether it is super-strength, deep-sea diving or living together in enormous groups.

STRONGEST

Gram for gram, the world's strongest creature is thought to be the rhinoceros beetle. It can lift 850 times its own body weight.

That's equivalent to a human lifting

60 TONNES!

ANT FACTS

In the Brazilian rainforest, the biomass of ants is roughly four times greater than that of all of the land vertebrates in the rainforest combined.

Although ants make up 2 per cent of all known insect species, they form at least one-third of all insect biomass.

The largest known swarm of locusts was made up of 40 billion insects and covered 1,036 square kilometres – that's the same size as the island of Tahiti.

40,000,000,000

The **GOLIATH BIRD-EATING SPIDER** has a leg span of up to

30 CM

and is the largest spider by mass.

Argentine ants live in enormous **mega-colonies**, one of which stretches for **6,000 km** along the Mediterranean Coast.

HUMAN FREE DIVER
273 M

EMPEROR PENGUIN
500 M

LEATHERBACK TURTLE
1,280 M

ELEPHANT SEAL
1,500 M

SPERM WHALE
3,000 M

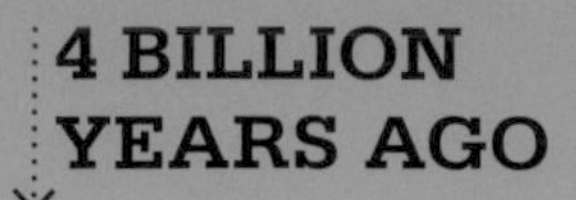

FORMATION OF EARTH
4.5 BILLION YEARS AGO

ANIMAL COUNTDOWN

Over billions of years, life on Earth has evolved from simple single-celled organisms into a wide range of complex creatures. On the way, new forms of life have appeared, while others have become extinct.

1.5 BILLION YEARS AGO

The Cambrian Explosion, about **540 MYA** saw an enormous expansion in life forms, including the evolution of **chordates** (animals with a backbone or notochord).

COMPLEX CELLS
2 BILLION YEARS AGO

Oldest fossils

The oldest fossils ever discovered were formed 3.4 billion years ago. They are the remains of ancient cells that lived at a time when the Earth was far warmer than today and its surface was covered with active volcanoes.

MULTICELLULAR LIFE
1 BILLION YEARS AGO

3.5 BILLION YEARS AGO

3 BILLION YEARS AGO

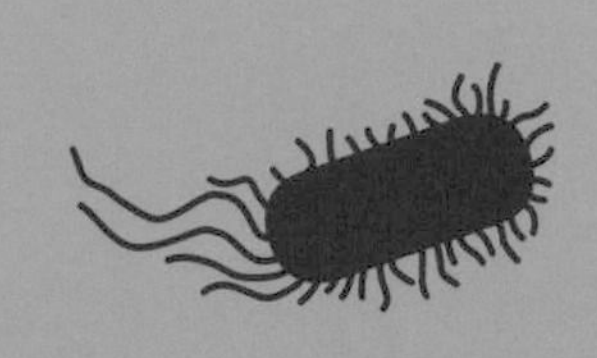

EVOLUTION OF PROKARYOTES
3.8 BILLION YEARS AGO

2.5 BILLION YEARS AGO

23:59

If the entire history of the Earth was condensed into just one single day, then modern humans would appear at one minute to midnight!

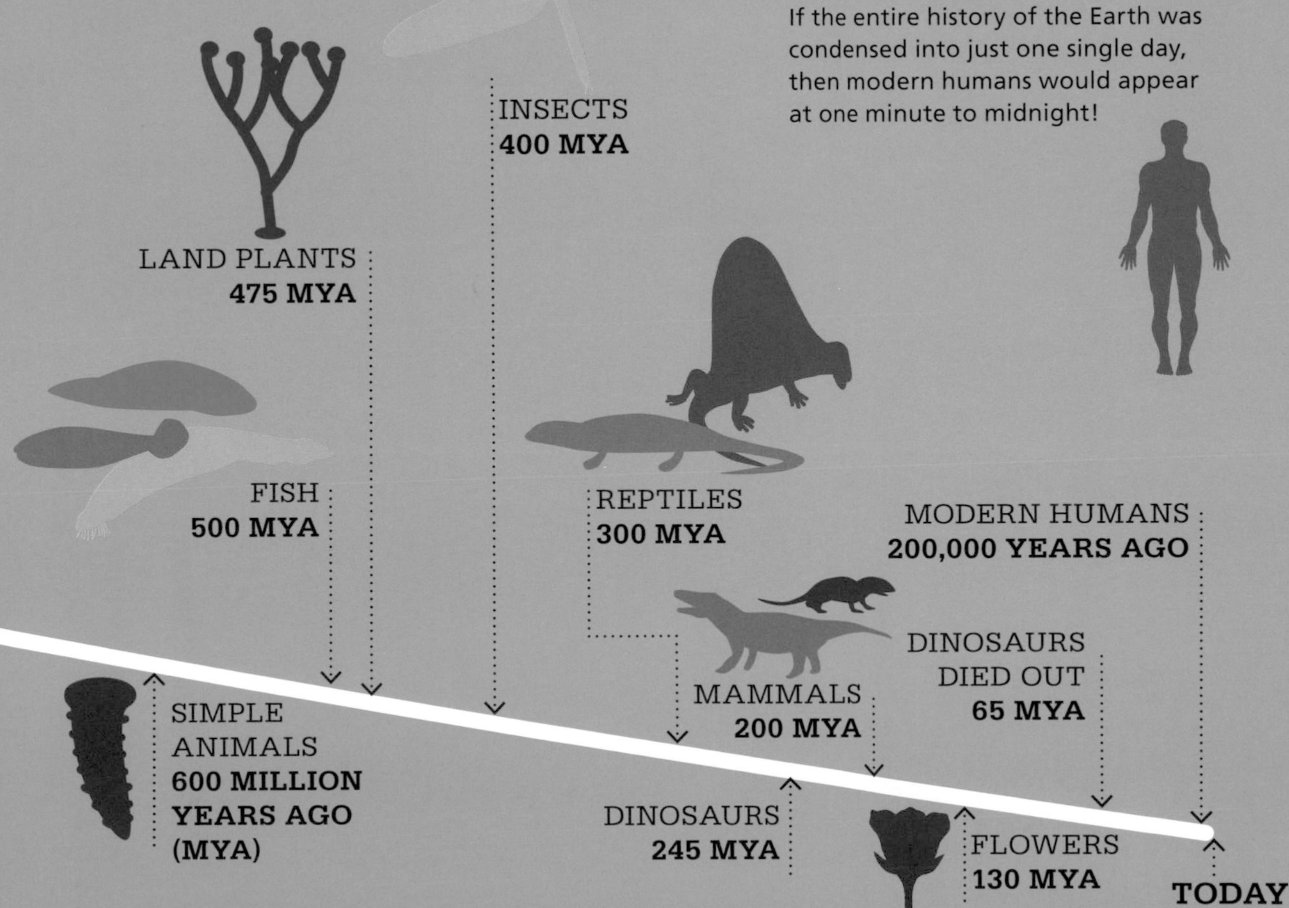

UNDER THREAT

Today, many plant and animal species are threatened by the actions of one creature – humans. With their ability to change and destroy habitats, humans are pushing many species to extinction.

20%

The IUCN (International Union for Conservation of Nature) Red List from 2008 shows that about 1,140 of the 5,500 mammal species, or 20 per cent, are threatened with extinction.

DEFORESTATION

At its peak in 1995, 29,000 square kilometres of the Amazon rainforest were being destroyed in a year – that's a rate of

3.3 SQ KM AN HOUR

or 80 square kilometres a day, which is bigger than the island of Manhattan, New York.

WHALE DECLINE

The pre-whaling population of the blue whale was thought to be

350,000

Today there are between

8–14,000

That's a fall of around

97%

SAVE THE TIGER

Figures from 2011 show an increase in the tiger population from 1,411 in 2007 to 1,706. This rise is due to the protection of the tigers' core habitats.

2007
1,411

2011
1,706

BORNEO DEFORESTATION

The area covered by rainforest on the island of Borneo (shown in green)

1950

2010

ELEPHANT DECLINE

Elephant numbers in Chad have declined from

400,000

IN 1970

TO
10,000
IN 2006

GLOSSARY

asexual reproduction
When something is able to create new versions of itself, or reproduce, without having to mate with another of its own species. Asexual reproduction can involve dividing or budding.

bacteria
Tiny forms of life that are made up of one cell.

biomass
The total amount of organisms in an area.

cell
The fundamental building block of life. Cells are able to perform all of the functions that are essential for life, including producing energy and reproducing.

consumer
An organism which feeds off other organisms that produce energy from sunlight.

eukaryotic cell
A type of cell that contains several specific structures, including a nucleus, which holds the cell's genetic information.

DNA
Short for deoxyribonucleic acid, this is the complex, twisting molecule found inside cells. It carries the genetic information that tells the cells how to perform.

evolution
The process by which plants and animals change and adapt to the altering conditions around them.

metamorphosis
When an organism goes through a major change in its body as it gets older. For example, a butterfly starts life as a caterpillar, before building a cocoon and finally emerging as the adult butterfly.

molecule
The smallest unit of a chemical. Molecules can be very simple and made up of two atoms, such as the gas oxygen, or they can be very complex, as with DNA.

notochord
A simple version of the backbone. It is a flexible rod that is found in some species and in the developing young of all vertebrates (animals with backbones).

nucleus
The structure found inside a eukaryotic cell which houses its genetic material in the form of DNA.

photosynthesis
The process by which plants use chlorophyll to capture the energy from sunlight, turning water and carbon dioxide into sugar and oxygen.

producer
An organism that produces energy using sunlight.

prokaryotic cell
A type of cell that does not have a nucleus to hold its genetic information.

respiration
The process by which organisms produce energy, releasing carbon dioxide and water as a result.

sexual reproduction
When two animals of the opposite sex produce young together.

species
A word used to describe organisms that can breed with each other and produce fertile offspring.

uterus
Part of the female reproductive system in mammals. It is where developing young grow before birth.

vertebrate
An animal that has a backbone.

virus
A type of organism that can only replicate inside another living being.

Websites

MORE INFO:

www.zsl.org
The webiste of the Zoological Society of London. It contains information on conservation and the latest scientific studies on animal life.

www.kids.nationalgeographic.com/kids
Information on the latest scientific missions, and lots of games and facts about the natural world.

www.nhm.ac.uk/kids-only
The children's section of the Natural History Museum website is filled with games, facts and information on plants and animals, both living and extinct.

MORE GRAPHICS:

www.visualinformation.info
A website that contains a whole host of infographic material on subjects as diverse as natural history, science, sport and computer games.

www.coolinfographics.com
A collection of infographics and data visualisations from other online resources, magazines and newspapers

www.dailyinfographic.com
A comprehensive collection of infographics on an enormous range of topics that is updated every single day!

INDEX

ACKNOWLEDGEMENTS

First published in 2012 by Wayland

Wayland
338 Euston Road
London NW1 3BH

Wayland Australia
Level 17/207 Kent Street
Sydney NSW 2000

Senior editor: Julia Adams

Produced by Tall Tree Ltd
Editor: Jon Richards
Designer: Ed Simkins
Consultant: Paola Oliveri

British Library Cataloguing in Publication Data
Richards, Jon, 1970-
The world in infographics.
The natural world.
1. Natural history--Charts, diagrams, etc.--Juvenile literature.
I. Title II. Natural world III. Simkins, Ed.
508-dc23

ISBN: 9780750269032

Printed in China
Wayland is a division of Hachette Children's Books, an Hachette UK company.
www.hachette.co.uk

the world in infographics

978 0 7502 6903 2

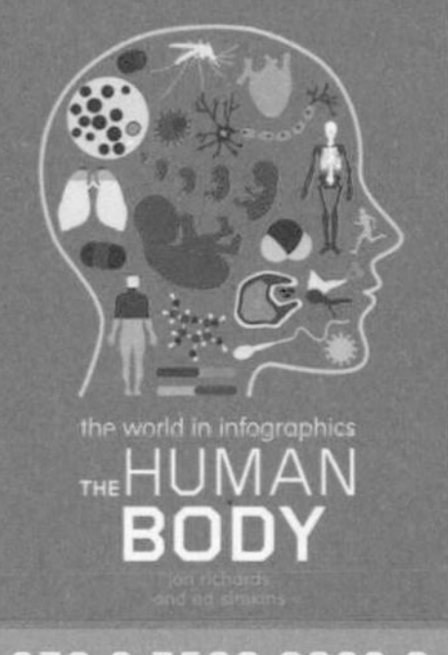

978 0 7502 6906 3

978 0 7502 6905 6

978 0 7502 6901 8

the world in infographics
MACHINES
AND VEHICLES
jon richards
and ed simkins

978 0 7502 6902 5

978 0 7502 6904 9

beautifully visualised information